Sports Fundamentals Series

SOCCER
Fundamentals

Danny Mielke
Eastern Oregon University

Human Kinetics

18318681
X

Library of Congress Cataloging-in-Publication Data

Human Kinetics Publishers.
  Soccer fundamentals / Human Kinetics with Danny Mielke.
    p. cm.
  ISBN 0-7360-4506-6 (soft cover)
    1. Soccer. I. Mielke, Danny. II. Title.
  GV943 .M49 2003
  796.334--dc21   2002015231

ISBN: 0-7360-4506-6

Developmental Editor: Cynthia McEntire; **Assistant Editor:** John Wentworth; **Copyeditor:** Nova Graphic Services; **Proofreader:** Sue Fetters; **Graphic Designer:** Robert Reuther; **Graphic Artist:** Francine Hamerski; **Art and Photo Manager:** Dan Wendt; **Cover Designer:** Keith Blomberg; **Photographer (cover and interior):** Dan Wendt; **Mac Illustrator:** Brian McElwain; **Printer:** Bang Printing

Human Kinetics books are available at special discounts for bulk purchase. Special editions or book excerpts can also be created to specification. For details, contact the Special Sales Manager at Human Kinetics.

Printed in the United States   10 9 8 7 6 5 4 3 2 1

Human Kinetics
Web site: http://www.HumanKinetics.com/

United States: Human Kinetics
P.O. Box 5076
Champaign, IL 61825-5076
800-747-4457
e-mail: humank@hkusa.com

Canada: Human Kinetics
475 Devonshire Road Unit 100
Windsor, ON N8Y 2L5
800-465-7301 (in Canada only)
e-mail: orders@hkcanada.com

Europe: Human Kinetics
107 Bradford Road
Stanningley
Leeds LS28 6AT, United Kingdom
+44 (0) 113 255 5665
e-mail: hk@hkeurope.com

Australia: Human Kinetics
57A Price Avenue
Lower Mitcham, South Australia 5062
08 8277 1555
e-mail: liahka@senet.com.au

New Zealand: Human Kinetics
P.O. Box 105-231, Auckland Central
09-523-3462
e-mail: hkp@ihug.co.nz

Welcome to Sports Fundamentals

The Sports Fundamentals Series uses a learn-by-doing approach to teach those who want to play, not just read. Clear, concise instructions and illustrations make it easy to become more proficient in the game or activity, allowing readers to participate quickly and have more fun.

Between the covers, this book contains rock-solid information, precise directions, and clear photos and illustrations that immerse the reader right into the heart of the sport or activity. Each fundamental chapter is divided into four major sections:

- **You Can Do It!:** Jump right into the game or activity with a clear explanation of how to perform an essential skill or tactic.
- **More to Choose and Use:** Find out more about the skill or learn exciting alternatives.
- **Take It to the Field:** Apply the new skill with in a game situation.
- **Give It a Go:** Use drills and game-like activities to develop skills by doing and gauge learning and performance with self-tests.

No more sitting on the sidelines! The Sports Fundamentals Series gets you right into the game. Apply the techniques and tactics as they are learned, and have fun—win or lose.

Contents

Introduction: Preparing to Play vii

Key to Diagrams xvii

Chapter 1 **Dribbling** .1

Chapter 2 **Juggling** 9

Chapter 3 **Passing** 19

Chapter 4 **Trapping the Ball** 29

Chapter 5 **Executing the Throw-In** 37

Chapter 6 **Heading the Ball** 47

Chapter 7 **Tricks and Turns** 55

Chapter 8   **Shooting** **63**

Chapter 9   **Chipping and Volleying** **71**

Chapter 10   **Moving Against an Opponent** . . **79**

Chapter 11   **Defensive Skills** **87**

Chapter 12   **Goalkeeping** **95**

Chapter 13   **Dead Ball Kicks** **103**

Chapter 14   **Offensive and Defensive
Tactics** **111**

Chapter 15   **Small-Sided Games** **117**

About the Writer 123

Introduction:

Preparing to Play

My personal involvement in soccer began more than 30 years ago. Although I participated in soccer activities in physical education classes and mastered kicking as captain of my second-grade kickball team, it wasn't until my sophomore year in college that my competitive soccer involvement began. In the spring, I showed up for the college team and managed to get several stitches in my lip during my first game because of an error in judgment: I got between a goalkeeper and a charging forward. With more experience in summer leagues, I successfully played two seasons as a defender, earning all-conference honorable mention in my senior year.

The natural progression from player to coach happened with ease. I have coached high school, middle school, college, and youth soccer teams for the past 30 years and have taught the sport in elementary, middle, and college physical education classes.

All these years have taught me that soccer not only is the number one game in the world but is evolving as a premier sport in the United States as well. Participating in soccer takes some preparation, dedication, and desire.

To begin a successful soccer experience, you must come prepared. Preparation includes the clothing and equipment you wear, some level of adequate physical conditioning, a basic skill level in the sport, and a willingness to learn new skills and challenge yourself within your personal physical limits.

Clothing and Equipment

The standard dress code and the equipment for soccer are simple. Every player must wear a shirt or jersey, shorts, socks, shinguards, and appropriate shoes (either cleated soccer shoes or outdoor athletic footwear). No jewelry, including watches and earrings, and no

A well-dressed soccer player—jersey, shorts, socks, shinguards, and shoes.

chewing gum are allowed during a competitive game and should also be avoided in a class situation.

Shinguards are mandatory in competitive situations and are highly recommended for any class or practice situation to prevent injury. The preferred style of shinguard has frontal shin protection and ankle support and guards, along with Velcro fastening straps. This model affords maximum protection to the areas of the leg that are vulnerable to injury. Other styles of shinguards offer less protection but, according to some players, may allow better feel for the ball and improved ball control. Socks should cover the shinguards.

Soccer-style shoes are specially designed for the outdoor conditions usually experienced on a soccer field. They provide superior traction and control not found with a cross-training or running shoe. The key to footwear is the fit: The proper shoe should "fit like a glove."

Another critical piece of equipment is the soccer ball. Soccer balls are sold under a variety of brand names, often matching shoe and clothing brands. Soccer balls can be made of high-quality leather, but most people use balls made of less expensive synthetic material. Soccer balls come in sizes 3, 4, and 5. A size 5 ball is used for ages 12 and up. Size 3 and 4 balls are smaller and are developmentally appropriate for small and young players.

Soccer can be played anywhere, but most teams play on a grassy surface with white chalk marking the lines and nets at either end. Goals are usually constructed of metal materials (sometimes plastic pipe) with nets that are typically made of nylon.

The only other piece of equipment that might be needed is a pair of specially designed gloves for the goalkeeper. Goalkeeping gloves provide cushion and improve grip.

Physical Conditioning

A soccer player's conditioning program should include flexibility exercises, sprinting drills to improve anaerobic conditioning, continuous running sessions to increase cardiovascular fitness, and strength training to develop the musculoskeletal system. Stretching, running, and strength training will make participation more enjoyable and help protect against injuries. Because much of the practice time during soccer class or team sessions must be spent learning and improving skills and strategies, each player is responsible for his or her conditioning throughout the year. The conditioning program has preseason, in-season, and postseason phases.

Flexibility Exercises

Stretching should take place before each practice or game. In team situations, the entire group should stretch together. Although there is no formal order for performing the stretches, typically you move from the upper body to the lower body. Before stretching, warm up with a slow, easy jog for at least five minutes.

OVERHEAD STRETCH

Stand with your feet about a shoulder width apart. Place your right hand on your right hip or thigh and raise your left hand high above your head. Your left ear and the left side of your head should come near your upper arm. Bend to the right and hold for at least 20 seconds. Repeat on the left side. Repeat the stretch in each direction.

TRUNK TWISTER STRETCH

Stand with your feet about shoulder width apart. Without turning your head, rotate your torso while maintaining leg and hip position. Extend your arms and keep them extended as you rotate, trying to point 180 degrees from your original position. Rotate slowly in a clockwise direction for about 20 seconds. Repeat the exercise in a counterclockwise direction.

CROSSOVER HAMSTRING STRETCH

Place your left foot to the right side of your right foot. Keep your legs straight but not locked. Reach down in stages. First, touch your ankle. Next, touch the top of your shoe laces. Finally, touch your toes. Hold each position for about 20 seconds. Reverse your foot position (right foot over left foot) and repeat.

CENTER "HIKE" STRETCH

Assume the position of an American football center—spread your legs, bend forward at your waist, and stretch your arms out in front of your body. Slowly walk your hands back in a straight line toward your body until your hands are centered between your feet. Reach back as far as possible and hold for 10 seconds. Repeat at least three times.

QUAD LUNGE STRETCH

Facing forward, extend your right leg in front of your body, keeping your toe pointed forward. Extend your left leg behind your body, keeping your heel flat on the ground. Bend your front leg about 90 degrees and hold for at least 20 seconds. Switch legs. Repeat twice with each leg.

MODIFIED HURDLER'S STRETCH

Sit on the ground and extend your right leg in front of your body. Bend your left leg with the foot touching the inside of the right leg. Reach toward your right foot, keeping your arms at shoulder level. Hold for 20 seconds. Switch legs and repeat.

BUTTERFLY STRETCH

Sit on the ground and bring the soles of your feet together. Grab your ankles (not your toes) and bend forward at the waist while keeping your back straight. Hold for 20 seconds.

Fitness Evaluation

Now that you have your equipment and the right clothes and are warmed up and stretched, it's time to assess your beginning level of fitness. To check current fitness levels, complete the cardiovascular fitness test (the shuttle run) and the flexibility test (the modified sit and reach).

SHUTTLE RUN

The shuttle run test measures your aerobic endurance. For this test, you will need two lines that are 20 meters apart (65.6 feet), and either a watch so you can check your time or a partner to monitor your pace. Run between the two lines, keeping the pace as shown in the table. Each stage is one minute. The pace interval decreases at each stage, requiring you to increase your speed. Continue until you can't keep the pace and are not within 10 feet of the line at the end of two consecutive tries. The initial time interval is 10 seconds.

SHUTTLE RUN TEST PACE CHART

Stage	Time (seconds)	Stage	Time (seconds)
1	10.0	6	7.5
2	9.5	7	7.0
3	9.0	8	6.5
4	8.5	9	6.0
5	8.0	10	5.5

MODIFIED SIT AND REACH

Sit on the floor with your legs straight in front of you. Place a yardstick or meterstick between your feet. Position the stick so that the midpoint (about 18 inches) is even with the soles of your feet. Keep the backs of both knees flat against the floor throughout the test. Lean forward slowly and reach as far as you can. Hold your maximum stretch for two seconds. The score is recorded as the distance before (negative) or beyond (positive) the toes. Repeat the test twice and record the best score. Compare your score with the scores shown in the table.

SCORING TABLE FOR THE MODIFIED SIT AND REACH TEST

Rating	Men's scores (in centimeters)	Women's scores (in centimeters)
Super	> +27	> +30
Excellent	+17 to +27	+21 to +30
Good	+6 to +16	+11 to +20
Average	0 to +5	+1 to +10
Fair	–8 to –1	–7 to 0
Poor	–19 to –9	–14 to –8
Very poor	< –19	< –14

Sportmanship

Before stepping onto the field, it's important to know the rules of etiquette and sportsmanship that guide the game of soccer. These 10 golden rules are from the FIFA code of conduct:

1. Play to win.
2. Play fair.
3. Observe the laws of the game.
4. Respect opponents, teammates, referees, officials, and spectators.
5. Accept defeat with dignity.
6. Promote the interests of soccer.

7. Reject corruption, drugs, racism, violence, and other dangers to our sport.
8. Help others resist corrupting pressures.
9. Denounce those who attempt to discredit our sport.
10. Honor those who defend soccer's good reputation.

Now let's step onto the field and play.

Key to Diagrams

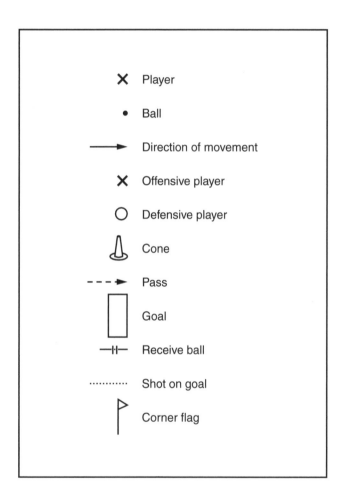

✕	Player
•	Ball
→	Direction of movement
✕	Offensive player
○	Defensive player
	Cone
- - -▶	Pass
	Goal
—‖—	Receive ball
⋯⋯	Shot on goal
	Corner flag

Dribbling

As you begin preparing for the game of soccer, the primary skill that will first encourage and satisfy is the ability to dribble a soccer ball with your feet. Most of us are familiar with the term *dribble* and often associate it with basketball. Dribbling in soccer is best described as controlling a soccer ball with your feet as you move within the playing field.

Dribbling is a fundamental skill in soccer because all players must be able to keep the ball within their control while moving, standing, or preparing to pass or shoot. Once players master the ability to dribble effectively, their contribution in a playing situation will be greatly enhanced.

Dribbling With the Inside of the Foot

In most cases, a beginning player will choose to control the ball by dribbling with the inside of the foot almost exclusively. As you mature as a player and gain confidence in your dribbling ability, experiment with controlling the ball with your instep and the outside of your foot.

Contact the ball with the inside of your foot, and position your foot so that it is perpendicular to the ball. Kick lightly to keep the ball under control and direct the force through the center of the ball, which will help you control the direction of the ball.

When dribbling the ball with the inside of the foot, keep the ball close. You don't want to have to chase after the ball because it is moving too fast for your skill level. Usually, you should keep the ball no farther away from your feet than one step length. Your step length

Make contact with the inside of your foot.

Keep the ball within one step length.

is the distance between your feet when you run normally. You can always increase the pace as necessary, but you don't want to lose control of the ball.

Always keep your head up, with your eyes focused on the field ahead rather than fixed on your feet as you dribble the ball. Work on developing your peripheral vision and feel for the ball so that you can sense where the ball is while you look at what is taking place on the field.

Don't dribble too long. Passing to an open teammate moves the ball up the field more quickly. Use dribbling to create space between you and an opponent, thereby putting yourself into a better passing or shooting position.

Keep your head up and your eyes on the field ahead.

Look to pass the ball to an open teammate to move the ball upfield quickly.

Use the laces or instep of your shoe, the inside of your foot, or the outside of your foot to control the ball. Where on your foot you choose to strike the ball depends on your speed and which direction you want the ball to go.

Dribbling With the Outside of the Foot

Body position is important when you choose to dribble with the outside of your foot. Your success will be determined by the distance between your feet as you dribble and your ability to maintain your balance as you push the ball away from your body.

Dribbling with the outside of the foot.

A good drill that will prepare you to dribble with the outside of your foot is side stepping, or sliding. Face forward. Move laterally (to the side) while keeping your body balanced and your feet moving. Do not cross your feet as you move, and use your arms to help maintain your balance.

Side stepping, or sliding.

Dribbling With the Instep

Usually, the instep or the laces are used as the primary kicking area for the dribble when you wish to move rapidly down the field. As you run, your toes will ordinarily point forward. As your foot moves forward, drop your toe and contact the ball.

Dribbling with the instep.

Dribble or Pass?

When should you dribble and when should you pass? The use of the dribble in a game depends on the area of the field, the proximity of your opponents and teammates, the condition of the field, and of course, your own skill and confidence. Often, young or inexperienced players panic and simply try to get rid of the ball. This practice could lead to a turnover.

The key principle to remember is that dribbling should be used to create space. You may need space to get into a better passing or shooting position or to give your teammates time to improve their positions.

Before you begin to dribble—in fact, before you even receive the ball—survey the field and determine the best strategy. The key is to plan ahead. Forward thinking and planning will help you make the right decision whether to dribble the ball or pass to a teammate.

If you decide to dribble the ball, focus on keeping the ball under control so that you can pass, shoot, or continue to dribble successfully. Avoid overdribbling or dribbling too long. Be skillful and wise enough to carry the ball only as far as necessary.

DRIBBLE TAG

Dribble tag is a great game to play to develop aggressive dribbling technique. Divide an area into a square 20 by 20 feet. Four players, each with a ball, dribble around the square. While dribbling, each player attempts to tag the other players without being tagged. The ball must remain within each player's control. A player scores a point each time she tags someone but loses a point each time she is tagged. Players should move rapidly while keeping the ball under control. This activity requires players to continually keep their eyes focused on the field of play rather than their own feet.

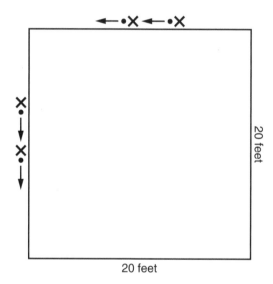

20 feet

SPRINT CIRCLE

The sprint circle is used to develop the ability to dribble quickly and come to a stop. Select an area on the field and mark two circles. The inner circle has a diameter of 10 feet, and the outer circle has a diameter of 30 feet. Each player has a ball. Players begin on the inner circle. At a signal from the instructor, players sprint toward the outer circle. When they reach the outer line, players stop, controlling the ball as they do so. Players should dribble quickly but keep the ball under control so that they can stop swiftly and still maintain control.

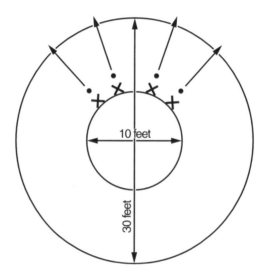

Juggling

The game of soccer involves teamwork, cooperation, and the ability to critically think through situations and possible options. Each player must have a wide repertoire of basic ball control skills. Juggling a soccer ball is a great way to develop quick reactions, ball control, and the increased concentration needed to successfully participate in the game.

Typically, juggling would not be introduced too early in the progression of skills. However, the challenge and thrill of success in this activity are great motivators for anyone interested in improving soccer skills. The ability to juggle a soccer ball successfully is a great confidence builder. When you can juggle repeatedly, you can create many opportunities in a game situation.

Juggling With the Feet

The ability to successfully and consistently juggle the ball demonstrates good ball control. The most fundamental juggling skill is to juggle with the feet.

To begin, toss the ball in the air or roll your foot backward over the top of the ball. This backward motion allows the ball to roll so that you can place your foot under the ball and gently flick it upward.

Keep the ball in the air by repeatedly bouncing it off your foot. Relax your ankle and point your foot. The touch—the force applied to the ball—must be adequate to keep the ball bouncing up but not

Roll your foot over the top of the ball.

Flick the ball upward with your toes.

so hard that the ball goes too high. Use the laces of your shoe as the point of contact.

Whatever part of the body is used to juggle the ball—feet, thighs, chest, or head—the key to juggling the ball is to cushion the contact. Slightly give with the feet as you make contact with the ball. This will create a softer landing with less rebound, keeping the ball close.

The kicking action takes place one to two feet above the ground. When the ball is at waist height, avoid raising your feet to waist level to control it.

Bounce the ball off your foot.

Keep the ball one to two feet off the ground.

You can use many parts of your body to juggle the ball—both feet, the thighs, chest, and head. The key to success in using body parts other than your feet to juggle the ball is to cushion the contact by using the principle of force absorption. Always let the part of the body receiving the ball give slightly as the ball arrives. This practice creates a softer landing with less rebound and will keep the ball close to the body. If you meet the ball like a brick wall, the ball will rebound too far away from your body.

Using the Thighs

Muscle allows more ball control than does bone. Raise your thigh to a position parallel to the ground and allow the ball to drop onto your thigh. With short, swinging motions, bounce the ball off your thigh while keeping it moving upward. Try to alternate between thighs.

Juggling with the thigh.

Using the Chest

Arch your back, forcing your chest upward. When the ball bounces off the chest, it should rebound slightly and stay in front of the body. Typically, the chest is used to control a juggled ball that may have gone too high off the foot or thigh. Chest control would then be followed by a juggle on the thigh or foot rather than another chest juggle.

Juggling with the chest.

Juggling with the head.

Using the Head

When you use your head to juggle the ball, always make contact with the ball at the point where your forehead meets your hairline. Avoid heading on the crown or vertex of the head or lower toward the face. Hold your position under the ball. The heading motion should propel the ball straight up rather than away from your body. Make contact with the ball by moving your whole body up toward the ball. Bend your legs and spring up toward the ball. Avoid being a passive header. Never allow the ball to fall on your motionless head.

Receiving the Ball

Another important skill is receiving the ball. Your juggling skills will help develop your receiving skill. Watch the ball flight or roll, and make a judgment about where it will reach you. Always play the ball aggressively and move toward the ball rather than wait for it to come to you. Decide which body part you will use to receive the ball long before it reaches you. Commit to your decision, move toward the ball, and relax the part of your body that will play the ball. Once you have received the ball successfully, quickly begin your next move.

Be aggressive when receiving the ball.

Footbags

You may find it easier to learn and perfect juggling skills while using a footbag. A footbag is a ball approximately two inches in diameter that is filled with rice, sand, or other similar material and covered with leather or cloth. In addition to footbags, other controllable objects can be substituted for a full-sized soccer ball. The Brazilian Futebol or the Takraw are examples of alternative kicking objects.

Practicing with a footbag.

Juggling in a Game

Juggling is usually regarded as a personal control skill, one that might more frequently be used during a practice session or conditioning activity. However, many times during a game the ball will come to you in the air rather than along the ground. Although a variety of skills could be used—such as a volley (chapter 9) or trap (chapter 4)—you should not exclude the opportunity to receive the ball and play it as a juggle. Keep the ball under control and await an opportunity to dribble, pass, or shoot. You may be able to evade an opponent by juggling the ball and lofting it into the air and over the opponent as you move around and retrieve your juggle.

If you choose to juggle, remember that you should take action quickly. In general, do not attempt to juggle if you are too closely guarded by an opponent. You need plenty of space. Make your juggle attempt purposefully. You might choose to juggle the ball to avoid going out of bounds or as a play after receiving a kick or throw-in. To juggle merely as a flashy display of skill doesn't make any sense.

JUGGLING GAME

Play the juggling game to improve juggling skill through a competitive activity. Everyone in the class or on the team has a ball. At the coach's or instructor's signal, all players begin to juggle the balls, starting with either a toss or a ground flick. Participants continue to juggle until only one person is still juggling. When the last ball drops, the activity begins again. Work on improving with each trial. Every participant should attempt to juggle longer each time the drill is run.

JUGGLING MARATHON

The juggling marathon improves foot-eye coordination as you try to complete as many consecutive kicks as possible. Use a regular soccer ball, footbag, or other controllable object. Using only your right foot, try to keep the object in the air. When you drop the ball, footbag, or other object, switch to the left foot and try to keep the object in the air using only that foot. When the ball or footbag drops, try juggling with alternating feet (kicking the ball or footbag from one foot to the other). Finally, juggle the ball or footbag using all legal body parts (feet, thighs, chest, and head). Set a goal of 100, 200, or 300 consecutive touches without allowing the ball or footbag to hit the ground. Keep your foot relaxed and try to contact the ball or bag below the waist. When using the thigh, chest, or head, remember to absorb the force and stay relaxed.

Passing

Soccer is truly a team sport. Although individual players with great skills can dominate under certain conditions, a soccer player must depend on each member of the team to make the appropriate plays and decisions. To create success within this team environment, a player must hone his or her passing skills.

Passing is the art of transferring the momentum of the ball from one player to another. Passes are best made with your feet, but other body parts can be used. You can move the ball more quickly, create more open field space, and generate more shooting opportunities if you can pass with great skill and finesse. Passing involves many techniques that are vital for keeping possession. Through good passing, you support runs into open space and control the game while building an attacking strategy.

Passing With the Inside of the Foot

Most passes are made with the inside of the foot. For the pass to be successful, the body of the passer should be square to the passing direction. This means that the shoulders, trunk, and hips are turned so that you face the direction in which you intend to pass the ball.

Once your body is square, draw back your kicking leg with your foot turned sideways so that the inside of the foot is open toward the ball. Keep your head over the ball and your nonkicking foot placed to the side of the ball to maintain good balance. Make contact with the ball on the inside of your kicking foot, which is the flattest kicking surface.

Square your body to the direction in which you are passing.

Draw back your kicking leg.

As you make the kick, keep the ankle of the kicking foot flexed and rigid. Follow through the kick by directing your leg toward the target. Be accurate as you direct the ball to your teammate. Don't kick too hard or you may overshoot your target. Don't kick too gently or the ball may not reach your teammate. Kick with sufficient pace for optimal control.

A common mistake is to attempt to pass the ball by swinging the kicking leg across the front of the body. This move decreases power and often makes the pass weak and ineffective.

Make contact with the inside of your foot.

Direct your follow-through to the target.

Use the passing technique illustrated in the You Can Do It section for simple, short passes of 10 to 20 yards that will probably remain on the ground. Plays that cover longer distances, such as corner kicks, crosses, or long passes 50 to 60 yards downfield, can be considered passes if they reach one of your teammates. You may choose to use longer passes to enable your teammates to outrun, outjump, or simply outmaneuver the opposing team.

You can pass the ball with your feet, head, or thighs—any legal body part. Which part of the body you choose to make a pass with depends on many factors, including the ball's height, the position of the opposing players, and the position of the teammate to whom you are passing.

Passing With the Laces

To pass the ball farther downfield, you must loft the ball off the ground. This soccer skill uses the laces of your shoe rather than the inside of your foot. Kick the ball below the middle to generate enough lift. In most cases, you should lean back slightly at the point of contact. Firmly plant your nonkicking foot slightly in front of and to the side of the ball. Extend your opposite arm for more balance.

Passing with the laces allows you to loft the ball, sending it further downfield.

Using the Drop Pass

Passes are not always directed downfield toward the goal you are attacking. One type of pass that is very valuable is the drop pass, which is made to a teammate behind you. This pass is extremely advantageous; it can create space and also catch your opponent off guard.

In a drop pass, you pass to a teammate behind you.

Using the Overlap Run

Another valuable passing technique is the overlap run. In the overlap run, the attacking player passes the ball to a teammate, follows the pass, runs past the receiver, and continues downfield to receive the ball again.

For an overlap run, follow the pass, run past your teammate, then receive the ball.

Give-and-Go Pass

Similarly, the give-and-go pass is an opportunity for a player to pass to a teammate and then run forward. The player receiving the pass quickly returns the ball to the first player as they move forward to another spot on the field.

The give-and-go pass. After passing the ball, run downfield and receive the return pass.

Passing With Panache

To be an effective passer, you need to develop the necessary skills through long hours of practice. Passing is a mental skill as well. You must keep your concentration and be alert to where your opponents and teammates are, in what directions they are moving, and where the pass should go to best create adequate space.

Consider passing to be a circular skill. In other words, a pass can go in any direction from the person initiating the pass. Often in the game players focus only forward and forget that they have teammates behind them or to the side. A drop pass or square pass can easily create time and space and allow the team to change to another part of the field where they may meet with less resistance.

PASSIMANIACS

The Passimaniacs game develops accurate passing and effective ball control in initiating passes. Mark off an area 20 by 20 yards square. Within this area, seven offensive players try to keep possession of the ball while four defensive players try to gain possession by getting the ball out of the area. Create space and keep the ball moving. Passes should be accurate; each pass should go to the intended target. When the offensive players complete 12 passes, they are awarded one goal. The defensive players score one goal each time they steal the ball and remove it from the playing area. Three goals win the game.

You can add a skill requirement by having the defensive players pass the ball out of the area rather than just kick it out.

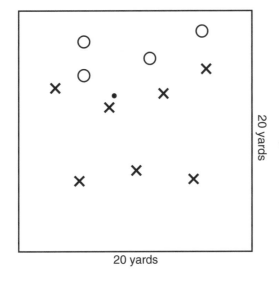

20 yards

20 yards

SOCCER GOLF

Soccer golf is a fun game that develops accuracy in both ground and airborne passing. Set up 18 cones to represent holes around the soccer field or neighboring space. The course should challenge players' skills; therefore, place holes on any terrain. Be creative. If a class or team is participating, use a shotgun start with players beginning from the previous cone. Begin the drill by sending two to four players to each hole (for example, four players start at hole 1, four start at hole 2, four start at hole 3, and so forth). Each player has a soccer ball. Players begin the drill at the same time, starting from their assigned holes. Players kick their soccer balls, trying to hit the cone. You can set up the course to have longer par 5 holes, with distances over 30 yards, or shorter par 3 holes, with distances less than 25 yards.

Players should use the inside of the foot and proper body position for short kicks. For longer, lofted passes, players should kick the ball with the instep, directing the motion through the bottom half of the ball.

Trapping the Ball

M uch of your time in soccer is spent moving around the field, creating space, guarding other players, and attempting to find an opportune place to await the arrival of the ball. You must be well prepared to receive and control the ball and to make an appropriate play that will benefit your team. Trapping the ball, whether with the feet, thigh, or chest, is a fundamental part of ball control.

Trapping With the Inside of the Foot

You can control the ball in many ways. As in other soccer skills, any body part can be used except the arms and hands. The simplest and most effective way to control the ball is by using the feet. Controlling the ball with your feet allows you to make the play more quickly.

In most situations it is best to use the inside of the foot (the instep) to receive and control the ball. This position gives the player the best opportunity to play the ball quickly by passing or dribbling immediately after receiving the ball.

Foot-eye coordination is extremely important. Watch the ball as it approaches and put your foot in line with the ball's path. You should be balanced on the nonreceiving foot as you await the ball.

Watch the ball as it approaches.

Make contact with the inside of your foot.

When the ball arrives, contact the ball with the inside of your foot as you relax your leg and absorb the force. By drawing your leg back at the point of contact so that the foot acts as a cushion, you absorb the force that comes from the previous kick and continues through the ball.

By absorbing the force of the ball, you stop the ball's momentum right in front of you, putting yourself in an excellent position to make a quick return play.

Draw your leg back, cushioning the ball.

Get in position to make the next play.

In addition to the inside of the foot, other parts of the body can be used to trap and control the ball. Three areas of the body are commonly used to trap the ball: parts of the foot other than the inside, the thigh, and the chest. The process is similar to that used with the inside of the foot. Absorbing the force is the most critical step in controlling the ball and trapping it accurately.

Trapping the Ball in the Air

Often during a game, you will have to trap a ball that is not rolling on the ground. A lofted kick or a bouncing pass will bring the ball to you in the air. In this case, it is likely that you will need to use a body part other than your foot to control the ball. Another alternative would be to raise your foot to receive the ball.

Trapping an airborne ball by raising the foot.

When trapping the ball in the air, use the same principles as you would to trap the ball on the ground. Watch the ball as it approaches and determine where you need to move to receive the ball. Position your body so that you are well balanced and in line with the ball's flight. Contact the ball, relax, and give with the force of the ball, absorbing the force. Drop the ball directly in front of you so that you can continue play quickly.

An important rule is to keep moving your feet until you make contact with the ball. This practice allows you to make adjustments to the trap as needed.

Trapping an airborne ball with the chest.

Trapping to Control

The objective of trapping the ball is to stop it and keep it near you so that you can control it. In a team sport like soccer, controlling the ball is key to the team's success. The more your team can control the ball, the more opportunities you will have to score.

The team needs to practice together so that all players are comfortable with the pace of each other's passes and so that they will gain experience in trapping and controlling these passes. Drills help develop skills, but eventually players must use trapping skills in game or gamelike situations. Trapping and controlling the ball in pressure circumstances is much different than completing a simple drill.

Secondary to developing effective trapping skills is the ability to anticipate the next play and quickly initiate that play. When you anticipate receiving the ball, think ahead and be ready to execute the next play. Failure to trap or control well and then continue play will result in frequent turnovers of the ball to the other team.

TRAP IN A BOX

If you want to learn to trap the ball and move quickly, try trap in a box. Using cones, create a square 25 by 25 yards. Players hold soccer balls in their hands as they stand inside the square. Each player begins by tossing the ball into the air and then trapping it. After trapping the ball, the player dribbles the ball quickly for five yards, weaving through the other players in the square.

For the first trap, players use their feet. For the second trap, they use their thighs. For the third trap, they use their chests. Finally, they trap the ball with their heads. Be sure to cushion the ball when trapping it. To increase the drill's difficulty, decrease the size of the square or require players to juggle the ball several times before trapping it and sprinting.

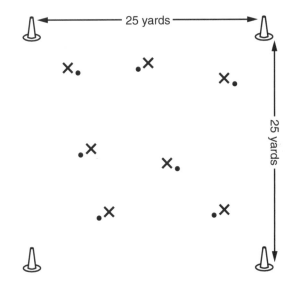

GRIDLOCK

Gridlock isn't just a frustrating jam on the freeway. The game can be used to develop accurate passing and trapping. Using cones, chalk, or tape, set up a grid pattern as shown. Two players, one passer and one trapper, begin the drill. The passer is in the center of the first grid. The trapper stands near the border of the second grid. The passer passes the ball to the trapper, who traps and controls the ball and then passes it back to the passer. They move to the next grid and repeat the drill. The passer and trapper repeat the drill in the next grid and so on until the end. Control the ball and pass it accurately. Ball control is useless if a player cannot successfully move the ball to another player.

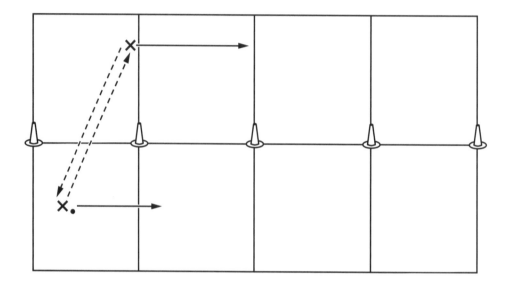

Executing the Throw-In

S occer limits use of the hands in game play. Within the regulation field of play, only the goalkeeper can use his hands and then only within the penalty area. However, when the ball goes out of play across the sideline or touchline, then a throw-in is awarded. The ball is in play immediately when it reenters the field of play, but the thrower can't play the ball until another player has touched it. A goal can't be scored directly from a throw-in.

Executing the Throw-In

The throw-in is one of the more neglected skills in soccer. Correct use of a throw-in can create many opportunities to control the ball and score during a game.

Before you throw the ball, you can keep your feet stationary or you can perform a running approach. When the ball is released, both feet must be in contact with the ground, either touching or behind the sideline or touchline.

To throw the ball back into play, grip the ball firmly using your fingers and thumbs in a spread across the ball. The thumbs and the first fingers form a diamond shape.

Both feet must be on the ground, either touching or behind the sideline.

Hold the ball with both hands in a diamond grip.

you can do it!

Bring the ball back over your head. Arch your back. Extend your arms behind your body. Bring the ball forward and release it in front of your body.

Follow through with your hands and fingers to control the ball and direct its flight in the direction you desire.

Bring the ball behind your head and arch your back.

Follow through after releasing the ball.

An effective weapon in a player's arsenal of skills is the ability to throw the ball a greater distance. A typical throw-in may travel only a few yards, but a throw-in that reaches from the sideline to the front of the goal is a terrific offensive maneuver.

The Running Approach

Use a running approach to accomplish a longer throw. Hold the ball with both hands, carrying it slightly in front of your head. Quickly run toward the sideline. Stop the approach with a long stride that places your lead foot close to the sideline as you bring the ball behind your head. Transfer your weight from the back foot to your lead foot, and forcefully thrust your upper body forward in a whip-like fashion. Release the ball at an angle that will allow it to travel the greatest distance to your target.

The running approach.

Pretender Throw

By the time the player throwing in the ball is ready, a second field player should be prepared to make a move. The field player should be approximately 5 yards off the sideline and 15 yards downfield from the thrower. The field player makes a quick 5-yard sprint at an angle toward the thrower as if to receive the ball at his or her feet. (This is the pretend part.) Instead, the field player makes a quick turn, changing direction and sprinting down the sideline away from the thrower. As soon as the field player breaks down the sideline, the thrower throws the ball, leading the runner down the field.

It is important for everyone on the team to know what is happening. The field player should use predetermined key words to alert the thrower (and the rest of the team) that the fake is on. For instance, the words "To my feet, to my feet" could mean to fake the throw. For a normal throw, the key words may be "Ball, ball." The field player must sell the fake, running toward the thrower with great gusto while using the predetermined words to call for the ball. The entire team must be aware that the pretender run is occurring, but especially the thrower and receiver must know.

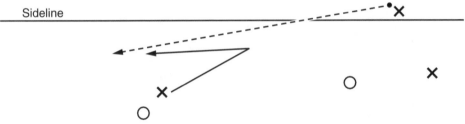

The pretender throw.

Trick Throw-In

When the thrower wants to get the ball downfield quickly but no one is in the proper position to receive it, an option is a trick throw-in. Two players stand very close to the ball out of bounds. One player picks up the ball as if to throw it in, but the other player takes it instead. Player 1 runs back onto the field and down the sideline. Player 2 throws the ball at the back of player 1, causing it to bounce back onto the playing area. Player 2, who threw the ball, reenters the field and controls the ball. The thrower must throw the ball forcefully. If the ball is thrown too lightly, it won't reach the back of the other player or won't bounce off hard enough. The throw should be a proper throw-in: Take the ball completely behind the head, use both hands equally, and leave the feet on the ground at all times.

The trick throw-in.

Tactics for the Throw-In

Throw-in tactics depend on where the throw will occur. In the attacking third of the field, the objective is to get the ball upfield toward the goal. In this location, a throw to a teammate in the penalty area is most effective. A throw to a teammate who plays the ball into the penalty area can also be worthwhile. The idea is to throw the ball in a way that gives your team the best offensive scoring opportunity.

In the middle third of the field, the primary offensive goal is to make forward runs in the direction of the goal. The player receiving the throw-in should be moving upfield toward the goal as she receives the ball from the throwing player.

In the defensive third of the field, you want to create space for a defender to clear the ball away from danger near your own goal. Overlapping runs and decoy runs are good ways to create space. In an overlapping run, players run toward each other, overlapping in the middle and creating a space where the ball can be thrown. A decoy run attempts to draw opposing players away from the player receiving the throw-in by pulling marking or guarding players away from the space.

THE GREAT PRETENDER

The great pretender game develops timing and technique for the pretender throw-in. Form two lines. The throwers stand at the touchline, each with a ball. The runners take their places in the field about 15 yards away. One at a time, the runners receive the ball, control it, dribble toward the goal, and take a shot. Players should practice proper timing, using key words or numbers to alert the thrower to fake the throw and await the cut and sprint down the sideline.

Use only proper and legal throw-ins. Take the ball completely behind the head, using both hands equally. Feet stay on the ground at all times.

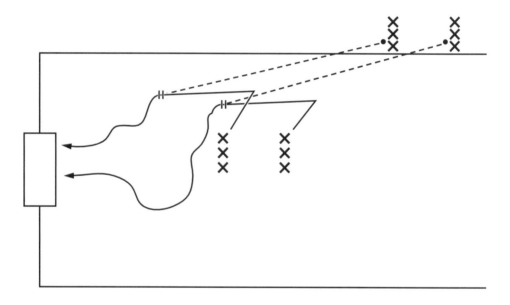

THROW A SCORE

The throw-a-score drill develops proper throwing technique and timing. The thrower stands at the penalty kick mark in front of a goal, holding a ball. Using correct throwing techniques, the thrower attempts to throw the ball into the goal. A goalkeeper stands in the goal and attempts to block or catch the throw. The thrower tries to be accurate and direct the throw to the corners and areas to make it difficult for the keeper to reach. For an added challenge, move the thrower back into the penalty arc.

The thrower can stand stationary or use a running approach. The thrower needs to remember to face the direction of the throw. The thrower can visualize that the target is a teammate and adjust the throw to high or low positions as would happen in the field during a game.

Heading the Ball

A unique feature of soccer is that the head may be used to play a ball in the air. A great deal of controversy surrounds play involving the head. Some research studies have shown that potentially serious consequences can arise from heading the ball. Although further study is required, the current recommendation is that young players not be encouraged to head the ball. Some authorities have gone as far as recommending protective headgear.

An experienced older player, however, can safely perform this valuable maneuver if he or she has received proper training in the correct technique.

Using Your Head

First, move your body into the flight path of the ball. This requires a good sense of anticipation and the proper timing. The process of moving the body into proper position is basically the same as that used with other ball control skills. Remember to keep your feet moving so you can adjust to the ball as it arrives. Inexperienced or younger players may want to use a soft foam ball at first.

Keep your eyes on the ball and your mouth closed. By keeping your mouth shut, you can avoid the painful meeting of teeth and tongue. If you prefer, you can use a mouthguard.

Move into the ball's flight path.

Keep your eyes on the ball.

Make contact with the ball on your forehead where your hairline begins (or where it once began with some older players). Keep your feet balanced as the ball approaches.

Always attack the ball. Don't wait passively for the ball to come to your head. Move your upper body from an arched position through the ball as it approaches. Typically, you will jump in the air when you head the ball. Using your legs, spring up toward the ball and direct it to the target.

Contact the ball with your forehead.

Attack the ball by arching your body forward.

You may wish to direct the ball back up into the air, head it down toward the ground so you or another player can make a play, or send it toward the goal. Sometimes you will need to make a diving attack at the ball.

Heading the Ball Downward

Using your forehead, make contact toward the upper part of the ball. This practice allows the force of action to push the ball downward. Remember to keep your eyes on the ball. As you head the ball, angle your force downward, keeping your head down and your eyes following the ball.

Angling the header down.

Diving Headers

Make sure that you are approaching the ball. Run toward it rather than waiting for it to come to you. Instead of staying balanced on your feet, dive toward the ball so that your body is in midair when you make contact with the ball. Direct the path of the ball by turning your head to either the right or the left as you make contact. During the follow-through, keep your hands out toward the ground and relax. Do not remain stiff. Hit the ground on your trunk (chest and abdomen) and slide along the grass to cushion your landing.

Heading the ball while diving.

Heading for Success

Heading the ball can be both a great attacking weapon and a deft defensive skill. The decision to play the ball off the head instead of some other part of the body is determined by the situation on the field and your position.

In the attacking one-third of the field, using the head usually means that you have an opportunity to shoot toward the goal or at least head the ball toward a teammate in scoring position. Flicking the ball with the top of your head is effective. A slight glance will send the ball a bit farther or redirect it toward an advancing teammate.

In the defensive section of the field, heading usually requires a forceful blow directed away from your own goal, sending the ball either out of bounds or back downfield. In most heading situations, two players, one from each team, will be attempting to contact the ball. You should assert yourself in being the first to meet and direct the ball.

A good way to improve your heading skill is to enhance your jumping ability. Winning a header may require you to outjump an opposing player.

THROW-HEAD-CATCH

Learn to work cooperatively with teammates to effectively direct headers toward a specific target or in a specific direction with this game. You need a group of eight or more players. Divide the players into two teams. One player on each team is the goalkeeper for that team. The remaining players pair up with someone from the other team so that each player has someone marking or guarding him. One player begins the drill by using a proper throw-in to get the ball to a teammate who then heads the ball to another teammate. The third person catches the ball with his hands and throws it to the next teammate, who attempts a shot on goal. If the defensive players intercept the ball, they become the offense and follow the same sequence toward their goal. This activity can be performed in an area of any size deemed appropriate for the number and skill of the players. There is no out-of-bounds area.

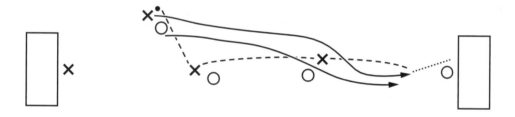

SHOT OF THE WEEK

The shot of the week hones rapid approaches to the ball and shots on goal. Set two cones 20 feet apart to create a goal. One player will be the goalkeeper, one the passer, and one the shooter. The shooter begins from a cone set about 50 feet in front of the goal. The shooter runs toward the goal. The passer stands to the side of the goal and awaits the arrival of the shooter. The passer tosses the ball, and the shooter attempts to head the ball into the goal. The shooting player should remember to use proper heading technique. Always attack the ball. The tosser should vary his tosses, requiring the shooter to adjust. This procedure is repeated 10 times, and then the players switch roles.

Players with a high skill level can attempt to kick chip shots for the shooter to head instead of tossing the ball to the shooter.

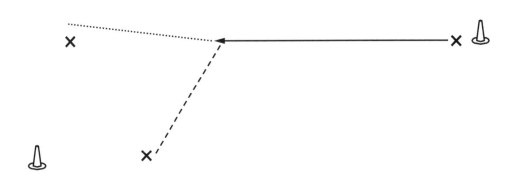

Tricks and Turns

Quick changes in speed and direction allow a player to avoid and beat an opponent. A superior command of basic dribbling and ball control skills is necessary in most situations. Frequently, however, more complicated skills are necessary to successfully deceive your opponent.

Several moves could be included in this discussion. The skills described in this chapter are generally beyond the basics you might learn early in your career.

The Bicycle Overhead Kick

The bicycle overhead kick was made famous by Pele and the movie *Victory*. Begin by facing the oncoming airborne ball. You want to contact the ball at a height about equal to your head height.

Jump backward and bring your kicking leg up. Keep your eyes on the ball as you continue to bring the kicking leg up toward your head. At the apex of your jump, contact the ball and kick it with the laces of your shoe.

Landing after the kick is very important. Cushion your landing by continuing the momentum and simply rolling backward, preferably over your shoulder. Avoid landing flat on your back.

It will take some practice to perfect this skill. If you are a beginner, select an area of the field that has some well-cushioned grass or use

Face the oncoming ball.

Jump back, bringing your kicking leg up.

a portable gym mat. First, just practice jumping backward and landing safely. Second, add a kicking motion to your jump. Third, have a partner toss the ball to you using an easy underhanded toss so that it will meet your foot at the proper location. As your skill improves, have your partner increase the velocity of the ball toss or kick the ball to you.

The most important component of this skill is timing the jump to match the arrival of the ball. Remember that force passes most effectively through the center of gravity of one object and then through the center of gravity of another. Contact the ball with the center of your foot, through the laces and through the center of the ball.

Make contact on your shoelaces.

Roll backward to cushion your landing.

The Maradona Move

This move is named after a famous Argentine footballer, Diego Maradona. As the ball approaches you, step on top of the ball to stop it. Next, step back off the ball and take a big sweeping stride so your body turns around the ball. Complete the turn with your body facing opposite your intended direction. Place your other foot on top of the ball. Drag the ball backward and quickly turn and dribble the ball in your intended direction.

The Maradona move.

The Drag Back Turn

Plant your nonkicking foot. Swing your kicking leg back as if you were preparing to kick the ball, but instead allow your foot to pass over the ball. Bring your leg back again and allow your foot to catch the top of the ball and roll it back. While the ball is moving backward, pivot on your nonkicking foot and lean in the direction you wish to move. Finish your turning motion and accelerate around the opposing player.

The drag back turn.

The Cruyff Turn

This turn, named after noted Dutch footballer Johan Cruyff, requires both ball skill and a bit of acting. You will exaggerate the movements, making the move easier to perform. While dribbling the ball, pretend to kick the ball forward but allow your foot to swing around the ball without contacting it. Place your foot on the ground and lean away from the ball. Use your other foot to push the ball back and behind you as you turn quickly and dribble in another direction.

The Cruyff turn.

Choose Your Move

Many of these ball-handling skills are extremely useful in the field of play. Try to perfect any or all of these moves. They will give you the edge in escaping and beating opponents.

Frequently, you will be faced with the need to evade a player on the other team. Often, your success will depend entirely on what move you choose and how well you can execute it.

There is no greater pleasure in the game than to challenge a player and effect a perfect Cruyff turn or similar move. Your advantage will set up passing and scoring opportunities.

Remember to choose your move well ahead of the need to execute it. Your choice may depend on the position you are in on the field, the position and skill of the defender, or your own skill level. The main thing is to try new skills in a game. Even if you are still learning a turn or twist, you should make an attempt.

NUTMEG CROQUET

Nutmeg croquet allows you to practice trick moves with control, followed by an accurate passing or dribbling move. A *nutmeg* is when a player passes a ball between the legs of another player. In this activity, two players team up. One player passes the ball to the other player, who then completes one of the trick moves (Maradona, Cruyff, or drag back). After completing the move, the player passes the ball through his partner's legs. (The partner should allow the other player to do this.) Complete a successful move before worrying about the nutmeg. Partners can switch roles at any time.

Another variation would be to set up a croquet-style course on which there are several players. Each player then completes a series of moves and nutmegs to finish the course.

Shooting

From an offensive perspective, the objective of soccer is to shoot the ball into the goal. A player should master basic kicking skills and then develop a wide repertoire of shooting techniques that allow her to shoot and score from many locations on the field.

Make the Shot

Approach the ball from a slight angle, not a straight line. Keep your approach steps short and quick. This technique allows you to make adjustments and plant your nonkicking foot at the correct location. Place your nonkicking foot or support foot about a foot to the side of the ball, with your toe pointing toward the goal. Draw your kicking foot behind your body with your leg bent about 90 degrees.

Swing your kicking leg forward to contact the ball. At the point of contact, your knee, body, and head should be aligned over the ball. Your ankle is locked, and the toe of your kicking foot points down.

Follow through in a straight line toward the direction of the kick rather than upward. Keep your toe pointed until you put your foot back on the ground. The momentum of the kicking action should carry your body beyond the point of contact when you land on your kicking foot.

Using short, quick steps, approach the ball from an angle.

Generally, a good shooter should remember a few guiding principles. First, keep shots near the ground. Although high shots are more dramatic visually, high shots give the goalkeeper a better chance to leap and stop the ball. This doesn't mean you can't use a chip shot or a higher ball as long as your kick passes above the goalkeeper. Second, try to aim shots at the far corners of the goal. Most goalkeepers will easily stop shots that come straight at them toward the center of the goal. Shooting at the corners requires a lot of practice and concentration. Third, use the field. A good shooting forward must approach the goal from different angles and positions within the field. Shoot from different distances and use different parts of the foot.

Plant your support foot to the side of the ball. With your knee bent, pull your kicking leg behind your body.

Shooting opportunities arise in various ways. Of course, a player can dribble the ball upfield while avoiding defenders and move to an open spot to take a shot. However, most shooting opportunities come after a pass from a teammate or a rebound off another player.

Shooting Off a Crossing Ball

A great skill to master is shooting off a cross from another player. The shot off a crossing ball can be played off the head, chest, legs, or feet. The shooter must anticipate the arrival of the ball and position herself to successfully shoot at the goal.

The first step is to know where the other players are—both your teammates and your opponents. Attacking players should spread out to avoid going for the ball at the same time. If a defensive player is guarding an attacking player, the attacking player must free herself by the time the ball arrives. The attacking player should be moving rather than standing and waiting for the ball.

When the ball is passed, the attacking player should be moving to the ball. The best opportunities to score will come when the attacking player has moved toward the ball and takes the shot with whatever body part is in the best position. There is no time to trap the ball. The shot should be taken in the air as a volley or a header.

Shooting off a crossing ball.

Moving Toward the Ball

Whether a shot is taken with the head or on a volley is determined by where the ball is located when it is received. Remember to watch the ball and anticipate its arrival point. You need to position your body in the right location to intercept the ball and direct it toward the goal. In most cases, you should be moving toward the ball and not standing stationary waiting for its arrival.

Move toward the ball when taking the shot.

Take the Shot

Often, players do not take sufficient responsibility for shooting. When you are in range of the goal and have an open shot, you should shoot the ball instead of passing it or continuing to dribble. Some players fear they will be berated for being selfish if they shoot too much, but open shots must be taken even if they result in a miss or a save by the goalkeeper.

Shooting is critical when the player and the ball are within the penalty area. Unless a player is blocked or guarded by a close defender, the appropriate action within the penalty area is to shoot the ball.

Statistics indicate that players will miss four out of every five shots they take. However, this fact should not dissuade you from making attempts. Never be discouraged from taking shooting opportunities. You will miss shots, but you will make shots, too.

If a player is going to miss, he or she should be prepared to recover the ball. A ball might deflect off a post or the keeper. Be alert to the possibility of a shot after a deflection.

RALLY SHOOTING

Rally shooting will give you numerous practice opportunities to shot and score goals. Set up an area of the field as shown in the diagram. The size of the field will vary depending on the skill level of the players. At a minimum, you need a square area 20 by 20 yards; the maximum size is 40 by 40 yards. A goalkeeper protects each goal. Soccer balls are available in designated areas of the field. Divide players into groups of three. Each group is given a number. At the beginning of the activity, all the groups jog lightly around the marked area. The coach calls out a number and a player's name. The group called attacks either goal. The player who was called by name gets a ball and provides a crossing pass for the other two players in his or her group. Players try to score using a variety of shooting techniques—headers, volley shots, or side volley shots.

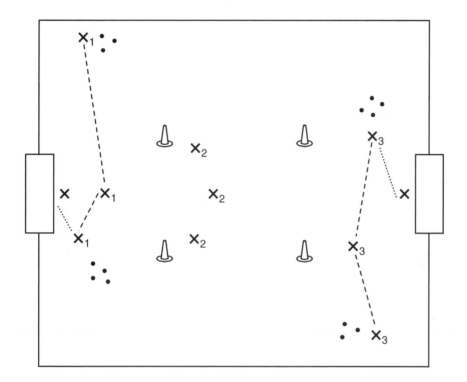

Make the drill competitive by keeping track of the number of goals made by each group. Note who scored the most goals or who achieved the most assists.

Adapted from **www.soccerclinics.com**.

SHOOTING AT THE BUS STOP

With shooting at the bus stop, you will practice dribbling and shooting at the goal. Mark an area 25 by 40 yards with two goals and goalkeepers as shown in the diagram. Divide players into two lines. Each player has a ball. At the coach's signal, the first player in each line sprints forward while dribbling the ball. As the player approaches the goal, he or she makes a decision on the shot and shoots at the goal. When the player shoots, the next player in line begins to approach the goal. After shooting, players retrieve their own balls and move to the back of the next line. This is a timed activity. The team scoring the most goals in a three- to five-minute period wins.

Shoot away from the goalkeeper. Use proper shooting techniques: nonkicking foot position, toe down, and follow-through.

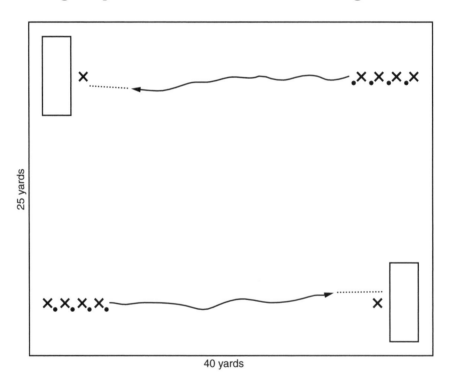

Chipping and Volleying

An interesting analogy can be made between chipping and volleying in soccer and chipping and volleying in golf. Picture the different loft angle of each of the iron clubs. As the slant increases on the club face, the shot will have a higher angle. When you kick a chip or a volley, your foot angle will similarly alter the ball's flight.

Volley and Chip

Both the chip and the volley involve either sending or receiving a ball in the air. Passing, shooting, or receiving a ball is best done while keeping the ball close to the ground. When a ball is in the air, it will typically be harder to control, which is why you might choose to use a volley or a chip. The chip is initiated off the ground, and the volley is initiated in the air.

For the volley, as the ball approaches raise your leg, leading with the knee. Keep your toes pointed down so that you create a straighter kicking surface. Keep your eyes on the ball and your head over your knee.

You can adjust the direction of the ball's flight by changing the angle in your ankle. Kick more toward the underside of the ball to increase the loft or kick higher on the ball to send it along the ground.

Volleying

Raise your leg as the ball approaches.

Keep toes down to create a straight kicking surface.

For the chip, approach the ball from a straight-on position rather than from a side angle. Bring your leg back using a shorter back swing than you might use with other kicks. Plant your nonkicking foot close to the side of the ball and point your toe toward the target. Contact the underside of the ball with your kicking foot and loft the ball. You may have a small follow-through or no through at all.

You can vary the loft by leaning your body forward or backward, depending on the desired outcome. If you lean forward, the ball will have a lower trajectory. If you lean back, the ball will have a higher trajectory.

Chipping

Approach the ball straight on.

Make contact and loft the ball.

Half-Volley

If you are in the wrong position for completing a solid volley, try a half-volley. A half-volley requires you to take the kick a brief instant after the ball hits the ground. This technique can be an effective way to kick the ball because it almost allows the player to tee the ball, giving it great loft.

The half-volley.

Swivel action.

Swivel Action

Some coaches and teachers recommend contact with the ball from the side. This action has been described as a swivel action. The swivel motion involves twisting the body so that when you move to contact the ball you create more force because of the increased body rotation.

Do I Chip or Volley?

There are a number of volley options. The volley can be used to make goals, clear a ball defensively, or pass to a teammate. Being skilled in volleys will aid your attempts at one-touch ball control.

Volleys can be used for passing. To pass to a teammate, the volley recipient must absorb some force of the approaching ball and lay it off to the teammate as a controllable pass instead of a wild clearing move.

Volleys can be used to clear the ball away from a dangerous defensive situation. Choosing to use a volley instead of attempting to control the ball may be a better choice in some defensive plays. The decision should depend on whether you have considered all the options.

Chips will be most effectively used in a game to loft a ball over a defender or a defensive wall, or as a shot on goal. As a shooting option, the chip is made from a free-kick position when it is assumed that the goalkeeper may not be able to reach the ball.

TRIANGLE

Three players form a triangle and practice half-volleys with each other. One player tosses the ball so that it bounces just in front of the next player. The receiving player tries to pass the half-volley to the third player. Focus on accuracy. Volley the ball where you want it to go.

PIGGY IN THE MIDDLE

The piggy in the middle will help you improve chipping skill and accuracy. This game requires three players or two players and a fixed object in the middle. The objective is to chip the ball over the player or object in the middle. If a player is in the middle, this player can be passive (just standing there as the other two players chip the ball over him or her) or active (trying to intercept the chip). If the player in the middle touches the ball, then the player who kicked the ball becomes the player in the middle.

As skill improves, players should try to chip over the middle player while moving rather than staying stationary.

Moving Against an Opponent

Soccer involves constant movement. Even when you don't have the ball, you likely will need to move to an open space, evade a defender, or mark another player.

Perhaps the most important movement you will make is that of moving with the ball while an opponent is guarding you. The main ingredient of success in this situation is to shield the ball from an opponent's charge or elude their charge by faking, also known as feinting.

Protect the Ball

When you are challenged, your initial concern should be to protect the ball so that the opposing player doesn't steal it. Position your body between your opponent and the ball, with your body forming a shield around the ball.

As the defender makes contact, continue to shield the ball by keeping your body between it and your opponent. You should probably

Position yourself between your opponent and the ball.

Turn sideways to keep the ball as far away from your opponent as possible.

be turned sideways, keeping the ball at the farthest point away from the opponent.

Don't hold the ball still for too long. After about three seconds, push the ball away and move to a new position, still shielding the ball.

Move away from the defender to a position where you can make a pass to a teammate.

Move to a new position while shielding the ball.

Move away from the opponent until you can safely pass the ball to a teammate.

Besides using a shielding position to protect a ball from a defender, a player can fake (feint) to elude an opposing player. The stop move and the zigzag (swerve) are effective maneuvers.

Stop Move

With the opposing player in close pursuit, suddenly speed up and then stop quickly. Use a drag-back turn, keeping yourself between the ball and the other player. If you do it right, you should throw the opposing player off balance and he or she will be unable to react quickly. Complete your turn and dribble in another direction or pass the ball.

Stop move

Stop quickly.

Execute a drag back turn.

Zigzag (Swerve)

As you approach the opposing player, drop your shoulder and lean to the other side, making it appear that you intend to push the ball across your body. As your opponent moves in to steal the ball, leave the ball "naked," or unguarded. Just before the opponent can steal the ball, transfer your weight, slide one foot around the ball, and push it away from the defender. Pull the ball away and move quickly in another direction or pass the ball.

Zigzag (swerve)

Drop your shoulder and lean to the side.

Slide your foot around the ball and push it away from your opponent.

Anticipate and Decide

Unless someone is sent off, 22 players occupy a soccer field during a game. This means that you will always have 11 players trying to stop you and 10 teammates trying to help you. Acquiring the skills necessary to maneuver in this environment is critical for success.

In a game, you should always anticipate what you will do. You have to decide to either guard the ball from an opponent or try to evade the opponent. It is always a good idea to look for an opening to pass to a teammate.

When you make the decision to move against an opponent, you may want to consider the following three elements. First, where are you on the field? Don't play around with the ball near your own goal. Second, where are your teammates? A decision to pass or try to carry the dribble depends on the availability of your teammates. Third, where are your opponents? If several opponents are close, would it be a good idea to shield the ball, feint, or kick the ball out of bounds? The decision depends on the situation.

18-WHEELER

Pair up with another player. One of you (the cab) will have the ball. The other will be the trailer. When play begins, the cab dribbles the ball while moving and shielding. The trailer tries to get around in front of the cab. Make quick, dodging moves. The cab has to twist and turn in various directions to prevent the trailer from moving in front. When the trailer gets in front, the two switch roles.

DON'T FEINT

Mark an area 20 by 20 yards square. One player is the attacker and one is the defender. The objective is for the attacker to dribble the ball past the defender, beginning on one side of the square and attempting to move to the opposite side. The players must stay inside the square. Players switch roles when the attacker is successful in reaching the other side. If the defender steals the ball, the ball is returned and the attacker begins again.

Use a variety of feinting moves to try to get past the defender. Generally, you will have an active defender who attempts to steal the ball.

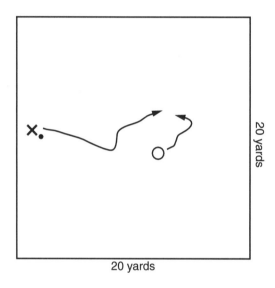

20 yards

20 yards

Defensive Skills

Numerous skills are essential for the success of a team's defensive play. Defensive players must possess good running speed and must be able to move quickly to various locations on the field. Defensive players must be able to guard or mark opposing players to prevent easy passing and scoring opportunities and should steal the ball from the opposition if given the chance. Defensive players must be adept at tackling, the action of using the feet to take the ball from an opposing player (not intentionally knocking them down as in American football).

In addition, defensive players must perform some essential defensive movements. Sometimes defensive players are called on to block shots at goal, clear the ball away from the defensive area, stop or delay the advance of the opposing team, or challenge all attacking players.

Executing the Slide Tackle

As a good defender, usually you want to stay on your feet while defending. Position yourself between the attacking player and your goal, then patiently wait for an opportune moment to block or steal the ball. However, if the ball is too far away to effectively block or steal, then you may choose to use the slide tackle.

The slide tackle is an essential soccer skill used by both defensive and attacking players. The slide tackle requires good timing and technique and should be used sparingly. Often players think that the only way to steal a ball from another player is to use the slide tackle. The major disadvantage of this technique is that unless the player can recover quickly, he or she will not be available for the subsequent play of the game. This may create an unfortunate mismatch.

Square up to the player you want to tackle.

Lead with the foot farthest from the ball.

To begin a slide tackle, lead with the foot that is farthest from the ball. This practice gives you extra reach and reduces the chances of giving away a foul. When you initiate the slide tackle, you should be in a position square to the player you wish to tackle. Your sliding action will be to the side, not straight forward.

Timing is vital, and the slide tackle takes plenty of practice to master. As with any soccer skill, watch the ball carefully, try to anticipate your opponent's move, and remember to go for the ball, not the player, when you slide.

If you contact the ball first and then the player, no foul occurs. But if you miss the ball and knock over the attacking player, your opponents will be awarded a free kick, which can lead to an easy goal-shooting opportunity.

Slide to the side.

Make contact with the ball, not the player.

Clearing the ball is an essential defensive skill. When you are in the defensive third of the field, you want to move the ball to the attacking third as quickly as possible.

Clearing the Ball

Be quick and get to the ball first. Be the first to reach the ball. Send the ball as high as you can to permit your team some time to get into position. If possible, it is best to clear the ball long downfield so you can initiate an attack. Often you can clear the ball with a volley or a header. Don't wait for the ball to drop and bounce before making a play.

Clearing the ball.

The athletic ready position.

Staying in Ready Position

Always be in an athletic ready position as a defender. Keep your feet moving. Use your arms to stay balanced. Crouch so your legs can spring when you need to move. Balance your weight over your toes so you are ready to move.

Developing Quickness

A good defensive player must be able to move quickly in any direction. To move effectively, push off the foot opposite the direction in which you plan to move. For quickness, move your feet in rapid, short steps.

An important skill to practice and perfect is the side step or slide. This fundamental skill is widely used in many sports that require a player to shuffle sideways. A great way to practice the side step is to slide from the goal box line to the goal line, side stepping 10 times. Rest and do 10 more.

Practice side stepping.

Using the Ball and Cover Approach

An excellent defensive strategy is to team two defenders in a ball and cover approach. One defender uses a solid defensive technique to guard the player who has the ball. Usually, the defender will be in position to close the passing lane toward the center of the field. The second defender positions himself to cover the likely recipient of a pass. Often, the ball and cover technique allows the defender guarding the ball to be a bit more aggressive in challenging the ball. The second defender also is in better position for stealing the ball when it is passed.

Shut-Out Defense

The main job of a defender is to prevent goals from being scored. Always stay on your goal side of the opponent. Then you will be in blocking position if the attacker shoots the ball.

A defender will need to block and tackle opponents. Watch the ball, not your opponent's feet. Challenge with your body turned sideways as you attempt to force your opponent toward the sideline. When you challenge for the ball, keep your weight centered, which will allow you to move in any direction. Use the inside of your foot to make contact with the ball.

A good defensive player is patient and does not overcommit when marking and challenging an opponent. Be ready to move when an opponent loses control of the ball or pushes it too far forward.

Be aware of your field position and the position of your teammates. If you challenge an opponent and miss, it may result in a goal if your teammates are not ready to back you up.

CLEARING

Three attacking players begin at midfield, one on each wing and one in the center. The three defensive players take position with two defenders and a goalkeeper. The defenders attempt to keep the advancing ball wide to the outside of the field. The defenders must be patient. They can allow shots from wide positions or cross shots. One defender should stay in the center of the field to eject any cross shots. The other defender challenges for the ball on the wing. When the defenders intercept the ball, they should clear the ball out of bounds or back downfield. The attacking players are awarded a point each time they score a goal. The defense gets one point for each cleared ball.

From a defensive perspective, this activity will show players how to force low-percentage shots and how to cover the center for crossing passes.

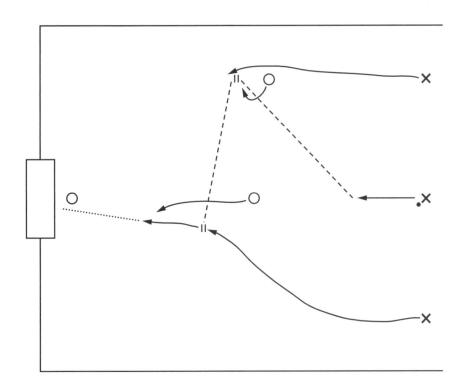

A CLOSING CHALLENGE

This game will increase skill in marking and challenging an attacking player. An attacking player receives a pass. The defender, who is 10 to 15 yards away, must rapidly close on the attacker. As the attacker prepares to touch the ball, the defender should assume a side-on ready athletic position, keeping the feet moving and preparing to react to the attacker's movement. Using short, quick shuffle steps, the defender attempts to get within an arm's length of the attacker. As the attacker moves, the defender stays goal side and with the attacking player.

Don't overcommit. Close on the attacking player and be ready to react to the player's movements.

Goalkeeping

Goalkeepers must have an exceptional range of skills and are regularly asked to serve as the last line of defense. Other players can lose a challenge or misplay a ball and be able to recover, but when a goalkeeper makes a mistake it usually results in a goal for the other team.

I have a personal stake in goalkeeping. My two sons have grown up playing in the goal mainly because they have displayed the integral goalkeeping skills of courage and determination and, as one of their soccer camp directors pointed out, "They have the heart of a goalkeeper." Although I can train someone to play the position, the aspiring goalkeeper must come with an innate desire to excel beyond personal expectations.

Get Ready and Catch

The goalkeeper ready position prepares you to receive the ball. Use a standard athletic ready position. Your feet should be about a shoulder-width apart. Your knees should be slightly bent with your weight and center of gravity slightly tipped forward so that you are standing on the balls of your feet. This position allows quick movement in any direction. Your arms should be relaxed and flexed at the elbows. Your hands should be in an open position with the palms facing the shooter. Your head and eyes should be focused forward toward the approaching players. Keep your hands up and open.

Goalkeeper ready position.

Absorb the force of the ball when you catch it.

The key to successful catching is to use a soft-handed catch. A soft-handed catch is much like catching an egg. When trying to catch a breakable object such as an egg, you keep your eyes focused on the egg and try to receive it by absorbing the force and cushioning the impact so that the egg doesn't break. Use the same principle to catch a soccer ball while you are in the goal.

After using a soft-handed catch to make contact with the ball, cradle it into your body. Bring the ball into your chest immediately after catching it. If you have to jump to catch the ball, keep your drive knee up so that you can jump higher and protect yourself.

Bring the ball to your chest.

You may need to stretch or jump to catch the ball.

Overhead Catch

When making a catch overhead, use the W technique. The idea here is to contact the ball with your hands in a W position. This practice allows a consistent method of catching. Typically, this technique is used whether the keeper is in the air or catching the ball to the side. Avoid catching with the thumbs pointed in the direction of the ball's flight.

The W catching technique.

The dive save technique.

Diving for the Ball

Whenever possible, try to move your feet in a side step or shuffle pattern if a shot requires you to move. Although a dive looks dramatic, it is less effective than pursuing an initial angle to allow a more stable save technique. However, sometimes you will need to dive to the side to stop a shot on goal. When diving to make a stop, lower your center of gravity, step in the direction of the ball, push off forcefully with your legs, and thrust your arms toward the ball.

Three-Hands Technique

If your dive to block the shot is low to the ground, you should use what is known as the three-hands technique. To get a feel for this technique, lie down on your side. Place your upper hand on top of the ball. Place your lower hand on the back side of the ball. The ground is considered the third hand. Your catch traps the ball to the ground and should prevent the ball from popping loose.

The three-hands technique.

Deflecting the shot.

Deflecting the Shot

It may also be necessary to simply deflect the ball by pushing or punching it past the net. This maneuver takes timing and practice and should be used with caution. If you miss the deflection or deflect the ball to the wrong spot, an easy goal for the other team may result.

You may use one or two hands to deflect the ball. One hand is most often used if the goalkeeper is diving or lunging to make a save. When the ball approaches the goal on a lob shot or a shot that dips toward the goal, the goalkeeper deflects the ball by using the palm of the hand to push or lift the ball over the crossbar. The goalkeeper's body should be turned sideways. The hand nearest the ball makes contact with the ball.

Use two hands to deflect a powerful straight-on shot. Push the deflection over the goal. Make contact with the palms and fingers on the underside of the ball, lifting it over the bar.

High Alert

Playing in goal is not easy. As goalkeeper, you must be constantly vigilant about what is happening in the game and make split-second decisions about how to play a ball as it approaches the goal. Stay on high alert throughout the game.

A goalkeeper must remember some key elements of play. First, you must learn to cut the angle of an approaching player. This means moving forward in ready position toward the approaching dribbler. From the shooter's perspective, the actual space available within the goal will diminish as you move forward. This gives the goalkeeper a better chance to stop the ball.

Second, the goalkeeper is the team's field general. Communicate constantly to the players in the field. Guide them on where to position themselves, encourage their skillful play, and alert them when a dangerous attack is threatening. In set plays such as corner kicks and free kicks, the players must listen to the goalkeeper's directions so a stronger defense can be set. When you move to catch the ball, communicate your intent and shout, "Keeper!" so your teammates know you are going to the ball.

KEEPER GET UP

Sit on the ground with your legs spread wide. Take the ball in both hands and bounce it on the ground between your legs. Bounce the ball as hard and high as you can. As soon as the ball bounces, jump to your feet and catch the ball at its highest point. Try to catch the ball above your head every time. Once you catch the ball, return to the starting position and repeat the drill. Repeat as quickly as possible for one minute. This activity will allow you to practice moving quickly and getting to your feet to catch the ball. To turn the drill into a conditioning activity, increase the time.

Extend your arms and grab the ball at its highest point. Use the W technique to catch the ball, always with a soft-handed catch.

KEEPER AND SERVER

At the penalty spot one player acts as the server with one ball. The goalkeeper stands at the left post, a ball in hand. When the goalkeeper tosses her ball straight up as high as possible, the server kicks her ball to the opposite side of the goal. The goalkeeper must stop her teammate's ball and then return to her original position to catch her own tossed ball before it bounces twice. Repeat the drill until the goalkeeper successfully saves the server's shot and catches the original ball before the second bounce. After completing the drill and resting briefly, the goalkeeper should move to the other side of the goal and repeat the drill.

To encourage success at first, the server should serve the ball near the goalkeeper and then gradually move the serve away from the goalkeeper and toward the opposite post.

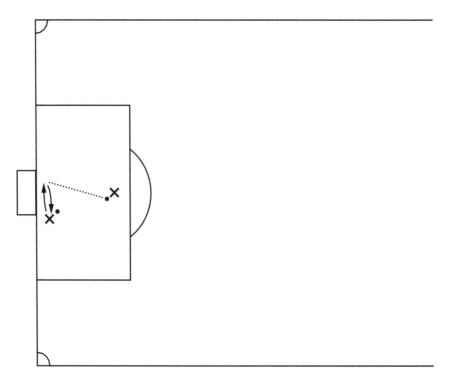

Dead Ball Kicks

Between 40 and 50 percent of scores in soccer come off dead ball kicks. A dead ball occurs when a player violates the rules and the referee awards the opposite team a free kick. The dead ball kick requires you to kick a stationary ball to a position on the field either short or long, low or high, with curve or arch.

Goal Kicks

Dead ball kicks include corner kicks, direct free kicks, indirect free kicks, goal kicks, and penalty kicks. The most dangerous of these kicks is the penalty kick, which places an individual player against only the goalkeeper. The other dead ball kicks should be practiced often as well. They can become dangerous scoring opportunities.

We will begin with goal kicks. When an attacking player kicks the ball across the endline, a goal kick results. Typically, the goalkeeper takes a goal kick.

Place the ball within the goal box. Run up to the ball from the side.

The ball must be stationary and placed within the goal box area. A short run up to the ball from a slight angle will add force.

Lift the kicking foot in a high back swing. Place the nonkicking foot slightly behind the ball. Lean back during the kick to give the kick more lift. Strike the ball on the lower half.

Use your arms for balance. Extend the kick with a strong follow-through to add power.

Make contact on the lower half of the ball. Follow through to add power.

Corner Kicks

When a defending player kicks the ball across the endline, a corner kick results. The ball must be placed within the corner circle. Place the ball in a position that prevents the corner flag from blocking your approach, kick, or follow-through. Try to "bend" the ball so that its flight arcs or swings toward the goal. To do this, contact the ball with the part of your foot around the base of your big toe, about where the laces begin. Contact the ball below the midline to achieve the needed loft. Approach the ball from an angle, lean back, and place your nonkicking foot slightly behind and to the side of the ball.

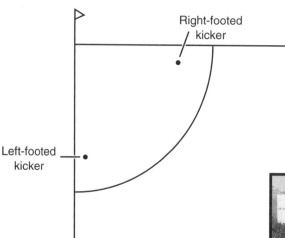

Right-footed kicker

Left-footed kicker

Position for a corner kick.

Make contact below the midline of the ball.

Free Kicks

A free kick can be either an indirect kick or a direct kick, depending on the seriousness of the rule violation according to the referee and the game rules. An indirect kick means that the ball must contact another player before a goal can be scored. A direct kick can be sent directly toward the goal.

In a direct free-kick situation, the defending team usually will set up a wall of players to attempt to shield one side of the goal. The kicking player usually attempts to bend or swing the ball around this wall. To do this, contact the ball with your instep at a point to the center right or center left of the ball, causing it to swing right or left around the wall of players.

The indirect free kick requires that another player touch the ball before a shot on goal. The first attacking player slightly touches the ball and allows the second attacking player to shoot at the goal. Another variation includes short passes from the first to the second attacker.

Ball contact for the direct free kick.

Making the Most of Dead Ball Kicks

Numerous strategic maneuvers can aid and assist an attacking team performing a free kick. So far, the chapter has highlighted some basic skill techniques. Here are some modifications.

First, instead of kicking the corner kick directly to the goal, the attacking team can surprise the other team by taking a short corner. The kicker passes the ball to an approaching teammate who then passes back to the (one hopes) unmarked original kicker. The kicker then takes the ball closer to the goal for a shot or short crossing pass.

Next, instead of bending the ball around the blocking wall of defenders, try chipping the ball lightly over the wall. This maneuver is somewhat difficult because if it is not timed properly, the goalkeeper will find it easy to catch the ball.

Another effective weapon is for one player to fake taking the direct kick by running past the ball. A second player then leaves and pushes or passes the ball to a teammate who then takes the kick. This deceptive play will often catch the defense unprepared.

In a game situation, using a dead ball kick effectively requires preparation. Lots of practice prior to game play likely will determine the success or failure of your kick attempt.

BEND AROUND

Place a cone in the middle of a straight line between you and the goal. Make contact with the ball on the outside center. Bend the ball to the outside of the cone and into the net. A larger object such as a softball pitching screen can be used instead of a cone. A goalkeeper can be added.

THREE PASS

A group of defenders forms a wall with a goalkeeper stationed in the goal. The attacking players get into position for a free-kick set play. One player stands in front of the wall. The player taking the free kick passes to this player and then moves at an angle to receive the pass back and take a shot.

Watch the force of the pass. The pass should make it easy for the receiver to take a quick shot. The decoy player needs to use a bit of acting to sell the fake to the defense.

Offensive and Defensive Tactics

For our purposes, we will look at two principal areas of soccer strategy: formations of team play and reminders of basic concepts pertaining to attacking and defensive play. The term *formations* refers to how teams align their defenders, midfielders, and forward attacking players during a game.

You and your teammates should decide which formations to use or which concepts to emphasize. A strong goalkeeper will allow more flexibility in your defensive alignment. Strong forwards might dictate a variety of strategies to utilize the midfielders.

The team you are playing against also will influence your strategy. Although your team may be comfortable with a certain approach, it might be wise to vary that alignment when faced with a specific opponent.

Field Formation

Defensive alignment typically uses four defenders, although some schemes have three to five defenders. My preference is to use four defenders: a sweeper, two outside defenders, and a fourth defender, the stopper, who works both as a midfielder and as a defender.

Midfield players are both defenders and attackers. Some time ago I heard that a midfielder will run up to six miles in a game moving from attacking to defending positions. Typically, there are three or four midfield players.

Your best shooting players and perhaps best overall ball control player should be assigned to a forward position. A forward should be prepared to take a shot from anywhere on the field and must be poised to receive a pass, control the ball, and shoot without losing control. Ideally, you have two or three players who can assume this role.

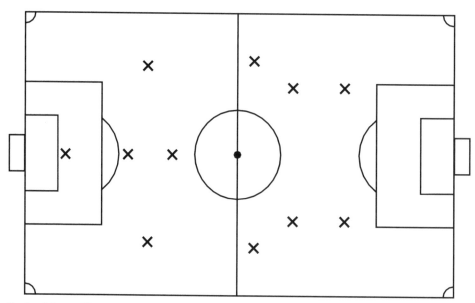

Typical formation.

The system your team chooses to play is also based on other factors. Ask yourself the following questions:

- What are our team dynamics? Will our style of play be influenced by how well or how poorly the team works together?
- What are the environmental conditions? Is it raining or snowing? During what season are we playing?
- What type of field—grass or artificial turf—is the game being played on?

The coach also has some vision of what the team should do. This requires that the coach know the strengths and weaknesses of each player and have a plan to engage players in appropriate positions and at appropriate times.

Team alignments vary tremendously as a result of team speed and skill, player dedication, coaching expertise, and the opposition. A variety of system options feature combinations (from defense to attack): the 4-5-1, the 4-4-2, the 4-3-3, or the WM. Any combination is possible, but the decision should be made based on the team's capability.

Combination options

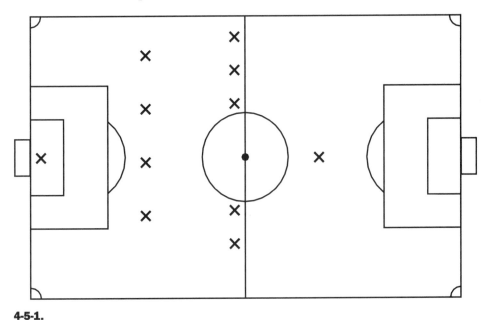

4-5-1.

Combination options *(continued)*

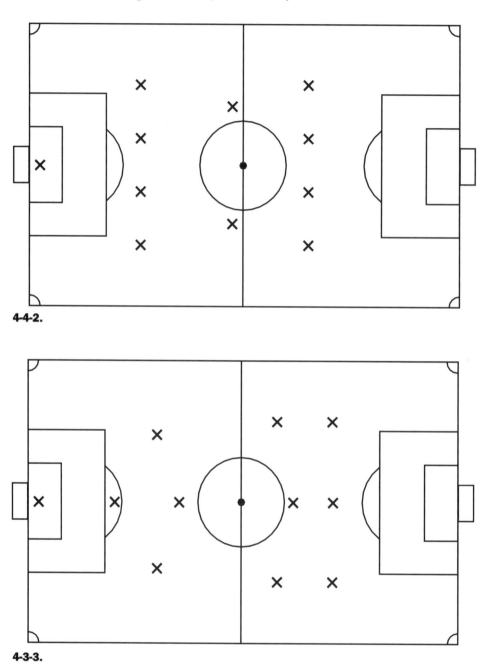

4-4-2.

4-3-3.

Tips for Attackers

Communicate with your teammates. Let them know where you are. Keep moving to create space for passing and shooting opportunities. Be accurate in your passes and select passing chances wisely. Beat defenders by using passing strategies such as the give and go, overlap run, or other types of passes (see chapter 3). Make your passes low and controllable.

Tips for Defenders

Always stay on the goal side of the attacking players. If you are marking a specific player, stick with your mark. Try to delay attacking players so that they can't quickly run past the defense and score an easy, unobstructed goal. Keep your feet moving and be prepared to shift position to guard an attacking player. Remember to play off the opponent and wait for the best opportunity to block or steal the ball. When in doubt, clear the ball out of bounds, downfield, or anywhere away from the goal. Understand your position and its importance to the rest of the team. Take responsibility for your area of the field.

ONE-THIRD DEFENDER

Set up two field areas, each 20 by 30 yards. Each area has a team of six players. Two players from each team are sent to the other team's playing area. These players are the defenders. The four attacking players try to beat the two defenders by passing and scoring a goal. There is no goalkeeper in this activity. If the two defenders get the ball from the attackers and complete three passes, one goal is subtracted from the attacking team's total. After two minutes, the defenders are sent back to their own teams. The scores for both teams are recorded. Repeat the drill with four new players acting as defenders.

Emphasize passing and receiving with the attacking team. Defenders should keep pressing the ball, perhaps using the ball and cover approach (see chapter 11) to prevent passes that will allow easy goals. In the ball and cover approach, one player marks the ball while the other player marks the potential pass.

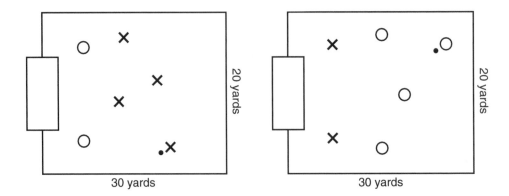

15 CHAPTER

Small-Sided Games

Once you have practiced basic soccer skills, the next step is to incorporate those skills into a game. However, a full game of 11 players against 11 players may not provide the best situation for either skill development or fun play.

Small-sided games provide the opportunity to play in any location. A small-sided game can be played in the street, in a schoolyard, at the beach, or on a smaller-sized field. Many outstanding soccer players have developed their skills in the arena of a small-sided game. The Brazilian soccer team, a world-renowned team, reportedly practice frequently on the beach.

Advantages of Small-Sided Games

With a small-sided game, you will have more ball contact and therefore more opportunity to enhance your soccer skills and techniques. With fewer players on the field, you are more likely to get the ball more often. With more ball contact comes greater opportunity for skill improvement.

A small-sided game will improve your concentration because you must keep the ball closer and make play-related decisions more quickly. You will have to rely on fundamental ball control skills such as dribbling, juggling, and passing.

Small-sided games are a fantastic way to develop and maintain physical fitness. With fewer players on the field, you must move to open areas quickly and create space for successful ball control.

A small-sided game can be organized easily. Small-sided games are easier for younger or inexperienced players to understand and have fun with. Sometimes too many players on the field or too many choices or decisions can disrupt concentration and skill performance. Having fewer variables on the practice field contributes to more positive play performance.

Small-Sided Formations

Small-sided games have a variety of formations. Depending on the purpose of your play or practice, you can choose any numeric variation. The most frequent variations are 3 on 3, 6 on 6, or 7 on 7. In most small-sided variations, the goal is six yards wide.

In a 3 on 3 small-sided game, the playing area should be about 30 yards by 20 yards. Usually, there is no throw-in when the ball goes out. Instead, the ball is kicked back into the field. Offsides is not used in a 3 on 3 game.

The offsides rule prevents an unfair advantage for the attacking player. An attacker is considered offsides when he is in his attacking half of the field with fewer than two defenders (including the goalkeeper) between himself and the goal. Offsides is considered when the ball is played and not when the ball is received by the player. An attacker who is in an offside position but is not interfering or involved with the play is not penalized.

COMPARISON OF MOST FREQUENT SMALL-SIDED GAMES

Number of players	Field size	Offsides enforced?	Comments
3 on 3	30 × 20 yards	No	No throw-in; ball is kicked back onto the field
6 on 6	At least 50 × 30 yards	Yes	Regular rules apply for throw-ins, corner kicks, and goal kicks
7 on 7	At least 50 × 30 yards	Yes	Regular rules apply for throw-ins, corner kicks, and goal kicks

In a larger small-sided game (6 on 6 or 7 on 7), the field should be at least 50 yards by 30 yards but a larger area could be used as well. Regular soccer rules apply for throw-ins, corner kicks, and goal kicks. In a 6 on 6 or 7 on 7 game, the offsides rule is enforced.

Strategies for Small-Sided Games

Small-sided games provide many opportunities to improve your skills, especially as part of a learning or practice situation.

When on the attack during a small-sided game, concentrate on creating space. Separate yourself from the defender, keep moving to an open space, and use your tricks and turns (chapter 7).

Assess the field situation often to determine if you should shoot the ball, dribble a short distance and then shoot, or pass the ball to someone in better position. The small-sided game also is good for reinforcing the need to move after passing the ball. It is critical to avoid standing around during a small-sided game because the area is small and players need lots of movement to better control the ball, pass, and shoot.

Defensively, you want to stop the player from advancing. Keep between the attacking player and the goal. Take the ball from the attacking player when you get the chance.

Avoid using the slide tackle or making an uncontrolled lunge in an attempt to steal the ball from an attacking player. Although a slide tackle may be appropriate in other situations, when you leave your feet in a small-sided game the absence of one player may result in an easy goal. Stay on your feet.

FIVE-A-SIDE

Divide into two teams of five players. One player on each team is the goalkeeper. You can use small-sided goals or full-sized goals, but small-sided goals are preferred. Use a size 4 ball or the smaller Futebol. The game is divided into two 15-minute halves with a 15-minute break between halves. Regular soccer rules should be applied and enforced.

Emphasize the advantages of a small-sided game—lots of movement, passing, good ball control, and quick shots on goal.

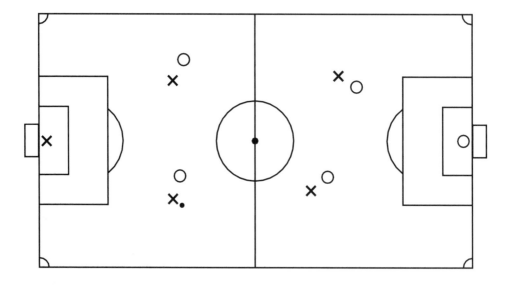

THREE-A-SIDE

The goal is a single cone or corner flag post. There are no boundaries and no goalkeepers. The objective is to control the ball, pass, move, and try to score by kicking the ball and hitting the cone or flag. You could also use two cones or flags to create a wider target. Because this drill emphasizes small-sided game play, two teams participate. There should be plenty of player movement and lots of physical activity. Emphasize passing accuracy.

About the Writer

Danny Mielke is a professor of physical education at Eastern Oregon University in La Grande, Oregon. Mielke has a doctoral degree in education with expertise in movement development. He has more than 30 years of experience in soccer as a player, coach, and teacher at the high school and college level and in 1994 was named the Oregon College Level Physical Education Teacher of the Year.

Sports Fundamentals Series

Learning sports basics has never been more effective—or more fun—than with the new Sports Fundamentals Series. These books enable recreational athletes to engage in the activity quickly. Quick participation, not hours of reading, makes learning more fun and more effective.

Each chapter addresses a specific skill for that particular sport, leading the athlete through a simple, four-step sequence:

- *You Can Do It:* The skill is introduced with sequential instructions and accompanying photographs.
- *More to Choose and Use:* Variations and extensions of the primary skill are covered.
- *Take It to the Court/Field:* Readers learn how to apply the skill in competition.
- *Give It a Go:* These provide several direct experiences for gauging, developing, and honing the skill.

The writers of the Sports Fundamentals Series books are veteran instructors and coaches with extensive knowledge of their sport. They communicate clearly and succinctly, making reading and applying the content to the sport enjoyable for both younger and older recreational athletes. And with books on more and more sports being developed, you're sure to get up to speed quickly on any sport you want to play.

The Sports Fundamentals Series will include:

- Soccer
- Volleyball
- Weight Training
- Basketball
- Bowling
- Archery
- Golf
- Raquetball
- Softball
- Tennis

HUMAN KINETICS
The Premier Publisher for Sports & Fitness
P.O. Box 5076, Champaign, IL 61825-5076
www.HumanKinetics.com

To place your order, U.S. customers call
TOLL FREE 1-800-747-4457.
Customers outside the U.S.
should place orders using the
appropriate telephone number/address
shown in the front of this book

Games for developing technique, tactics, and team play

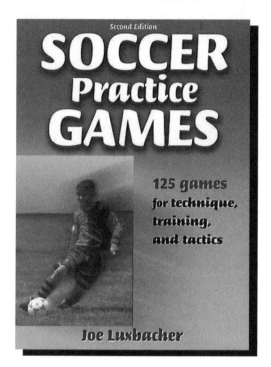

Second Edition

SOCCER Practice GAMES

125 games for technique, training, and tactics

Joe Luxbacher

2003 • 160 pages • ISBN 0-7360-4789-1

Make each practice more challenging, productive, and fun with 125 games! Divided into six sections, *Soccer Practice Games* presents games on the following aspects:

- Warm-up and conditioning
- Passing and receiving
- Dribbling, shielding, and tackling
- Heading and shooting
- Tactical training
- Goalkeeper training

Each game maximizes player involvement, activity, and learning and contains at least one major objective related to player or team development. A detailed explanation and accompanying illustrations are provided for each game to make application easy. Games can be easily adapted to accommodate players of various ages and abilities.

Designed for beginning youth through high school competitive levels, *Soccer Practice Games* is a big winner among coaches and those who teach soccer. Whether working with whole teams, small groups, or players one-on-one, it is a fun and effective way to instruct and learn the game.

HUMAN KINETICS
The Premier Publisher for Sports & Fitness
P.O. Box 5076, Champaign, IL 61825-5076
www.HumanKinetics.com

To place your order, U.S. customers call
TOLL FREE 1-800-747-4457.
Customers outside the U.S. should place orders using the appropriate telephone number/address shown in the front of this book